Ocean
of Silence

Also by Billy Doyle

The Mirage of Separation
Yoga in the Kashmir Tradition

OCEAN
OF SILENCE

Billy Doyle

NEW SARUM PRESS
UNITED KINGDOM

First published May 2022 by New Sarum Press

© Billy Doyle 2022
Billy Doyle has asserted his right under the Copyright, Designs and Patents
Act, 1988, to be identified as author of this work.

Typeset in Dante 12/16 & Syntax 11/16

New Sarum Press, Salisbury, SP2 8JP
United Kingdom

ISBN: 978-1-7397249-1-7

www.newsarumpress.com

"If we disinterestedly observe the arising and disappearing of all the states we experience, we soon come to realize that each state, each perception, each thought, is reabsorbed into an unspoken knowing, knowing as being. This, the continuum, the only reality, is there before activity commences. Let yourself sink deep within this stillness each time it makes itself felt."

Jean Klein, *I Am*

Introduction

Our real nature, consciousness, is beyond the mind to grasp and yet it is our most intimate reality.

When we objectify ourselves, identifying with an image, memory or individual personality, we lose sight of our real nature. We become engrossed in a world of objects and an endless cycle of pleasure and pain.

Only through a deep self-inquiry do we come to understand we are not the body-mind, for it too is a perception in awareness, but we are awareness itself, beyond the personal.

We are no longer time bound, but time and space are within us. The outer and inner division dissolves.

The writings in this book are pointers to this non-dual reality.

Billy Doyle
May 2022

Index of first lines

Ocean of Silence

to hear the sound of the poplar tree in the soft breeze

the wings of the dragonfly fluttering by

the water droplet on the pond

the cry of the owl in the night

the beat of your heart

the mind has to come to stillness

perhaps then you can hear the sound of the Self

the soundless sound

pervading the universe

look out at the open landscape
or imagine one spreading endlessly in front of you
enter into it
touch it, embrace it with your whole being
let it absorb you
there are not two

this very moment
have you ever dived into its depth
or are you forever taken by the waves of your mind
here, now, the whole universe is open to you
singing its song
but if you're not quiet
all you will hear is your own echo

finally at home
no key to the door
no door, no walls or roof
at home in infinite space
in the eternity
why not meet me here
you ask the address
everywhere and anywhere

don't try to travel there
even with wings you won't arrive
nonsense to think a phantom
will reach the apex
don't you see you are just a dream world
what's never been lost
will never be found
what's never left home
will never return

nothingness, emptiness
it seems a dark forlorn place
but have you ever taken a peek inside
entered and examined its domain
you might be surprised with what you discover
a love and joy you have always run away from
frightened you would dissolve

with grasping eyes
it will never be yours
you may acquire the world
but still you'll be a beggar
what you really want is nothing
but nothingness is a precious gift
you have to be worthy of it
first your eyes have to turn inwards
in the darkness there is light

feel yourself oceanic
let all the bubbles pass through you
every current, motion and wave are your expression
feel yourself cosmic
the world, stars and galaxies have their life in you
feel yourself infinite
you breathe forth time and space

the wave jumps from the sea
seeking its independence
expressing its individuality
fighting to be free
but one day exhausted from its endeavours
and in the quiet shallows
it settles back into the sea
it finds a different reality
one with the sea, one with the ocean
and realises no matter what the expression
all is ultimately water

you are the silence
not what appears in the silence
you are the seeing
not what is seen
you are the listening
not what is listened to
you are the life
not what is lived
you are no-thing
so let the manifest go
now see you are also what appears in the silence
the seeing, the listening
there are never two

10

all is the Self
have you ever experienced anything other than the Self
have you ever seen anything that is not the Self
have you ever heard anything other than the Self
there is no other
there are never two

the idea I am the body has embedded itself
deep in the confines of your body
in your cells, in your eyes, in your lungs
in the pathways of your brain
give space to your body
let yourself breathe
unthink the mind
let the thoughts die back from whence they arose
discover yourself here, beyond all form

let the exhale die
wait in that eternity for the inhale
let it come to you
let it breathe you
be an open space for the breath
surrender with the out-breath
let yourself dissolve
let your whole body, every cell
be permeated by the in-breath
feel your breathing in the space around you
there is nobody breathing
and there is only breathing

with your vision always on the horizon
do you ever behold the sacredness
in front of your eyes
always with tomorrow
sacrificing the only reality
living in your illusion
dead to here and now

try living a day, or a morning, or even a few minutes
without the me thought
pure seeing, pure hearing
liberated from that controller, judge and analyser

the cry of the children
playing in the park
running into the sunlight
the screams of joy
dancing through the leaves
the exuberance of life
the ecstasy whirling in the breeze

dancing tree branches
I'm dancing with you
hand in hand
branch in branch
swaying this way
whirling the other
open to the heavens
a joy forever

you can bury your anger
stamp it underground
but the seed will not perish
one day it will sprout forth
overwhelm you
why not make friends with it
give it the light of day
it has much to tell you

it's not the wolf you imagine
don't fear fear
welcome it with open arms
feel it in your stomach
to the tips of your fingers
let it flow through you
give it no hold
let it die in your acceptance

there is always hope
there is always a tomorrow
always an escape
to lure you away
what if there were no time
no tomorrow
only the present to see
only presence

the limits you impose on yourself
are those of time and space
what is time
a mind creation, a thought
what is space
a mind creation, a perception
free of thought and perception
you come to the limitless reality

deep sleep
feel its fragrance on awakening
silently contemplate its nature
does it have shape, colour or duration
any memory or history
any sorrow or pain
now contemplate pure consciousness

on waking, stop
don't be too quick to jump
to a world of objects
remember where you've been
the peace of deep sleep
feel its scent
where you possessed nothing
not even a thought
yet, you would not sacrifice it
can you find the deep sleep state here, now
with nothing possessed
as you walk through this world

discover your transparency
then the insult does not register
the blow never lands
all passes through you as through thin air
be it praise or blame
who is there to care
fearless you walk life

without the I
where is fear
with no inside or outside
what is there to fear
and who is there to fear
I am all that is
and one with all

the world out there is real, isn't it
but what world are you talking about
the world of the bumble bee, the owl
the chimpanzee, the worm, your world
or that of an extra-terrestrial being
the world is just your senses
your senses are your mind
so the world is just mind
mind is consciousness
you are consciousness
as is the world

consciousness evolved from a single cell creature
you can't be serious!
there's a world out there independent of consciousness
is that so
consciousness was born and will die
believe it if you will
but consciousness is laughing at you

this moment, this breath
a planet like no other
a body millions of years in the making
this gift of life
but do we respect it
when we pollute our bodies
our brains, our environment
where is our thankfulness!

it may all be an illusion
the streamers of aurora borealis shimmering
the dance of the butterflies intertwining in the air
the stately emergence of the elephants from the jungle
the sycamore seeds swirling through the breeze
the colours of the coral reef
the peacock's enticing display
but what an illusion

at the end of the exhale

silence

after the cry of the blackbird

silence

after the siren of the ambulance

silence

after the scent of the jasmine has wafted away

silence

always waiting for you

thought arises and subsides back into silence

the breath rises and falls back into silence

all that is perceived, every object

comes into consciousness and dissolves in consciousness

silence, consciousness, is the background

of all that arises and dies

but what arises and dissolves in consciousness

is not other than consciousness

in reality there is nothing other than consciousness

you may think reality is elusive
but only because you think
you could see it, touch it
but it's much too close
it's before you see
before you touch or even think
search all you like
one day when exhausted
you'll know it as yourself
that you never lost

the pilgrimage to the sacred is no journey
yet it will take every gram of your being
it's closer than close
yet it may take a lifetime to unveil
but the walls you have built
may crumble at any moment
they are but shadows in the mind

who is there to die
only an expression of life
time for it to come to rest
birth and death are its cycle
life was not born and does not die
you're not a collection of cells belonging to time
but life itself

34

your teacher has passed away
but why this despondency
truth does not pass away
her words are to set you free
free too from the teacher
free from birth and death
let the words resonate more deeply
into silence

tick tock, tick tock

a world of endless change

the crest and trough of the wave

from famine to plenty, from health to sickness

but is there not an underlying reality

a changeless foundation

beyond security and insecurity

it is the Self

like the ocean identifying with a wave
like the universe thinking itself
to be a speck of cloud dust
eternity thinking itself
a few tick tocks of a clock
you, Consciousness itself
taking yourself for a mere object

when you come to the deep conviction of what you're not
body, senses or mind
you are open to a deeper dimension beyond the mind
and when this reality blossoms
it's not that you come to understand something new
rather all ideas of what you are disappear
there's only
space
openness
welcoming
love
the end of all division

after coming to understand
I'm not the body, the mind or any object
don't stop there, go further
see you are also the body and mind
and every object
that the void is fullness
and that all is indeed sacred

will you ever come to know me
until you know yourself
you will never come to know me
otherwise we are just surfaces meeting
not even that
just illusions
passing in a dream
when we really wake up
there is no other to know

I stand as myself, naked
though I was never born
I walk through life rich but I have no acquisitions
I speak many tongues
you can hear me in the blackbird singing on the rooftop
the child roaring with laughter
I have many colours
the green leaves of spring
the crimson of the peony
I walk through many foreign lands
but you'll always find me at home
you can see through me, I'm completely transparent
when we finally meet
you'll know me as an old friend

you're just a shadow of yourself
the shadow appears to have a reality
it has form and movement
you take yourself for a mere image
but shadow and substance are of a different order
remove the illusory mind
and the long shadow it casts disappears
when the sun is overhead, where is the shadow
when truth is overhead there is no shadow
only the light

how could you possibly think
that objects are somehow outside
and independent of consciousness
consciousness infuses all its creation with its own nature
in love there is never two, there is no other
the beloved is not other than love itself
there is no escape for an object to exist independently
all that is beheld in love is only one

the infinite loses itself in the finite
it becomes a buttercup, a sea anemone
a robin, a human, a galaxy
but if you investigate these expressions
remove the layers and look underneath
you won't find any object
you will only come back every time to the infinite
that every apparent object is celebrating

the thought comes from silence
and dissolves back into silence
the breath comes from silence
and dies back into silence
the emotion arises in silence
and fades back into silence
the twang of the sitar comes out of silence
and fades away into silence
the sun rises in silence
and sets back into silence
but Silence does not arise or set
it ever is

are you quite sure you want to pursue this path
to arrive at the non-existence of yourself
to leave behind all you hold dear
of who you think you are
are you ready to die to all your notions
ready to be nobody
to jump without a parachute

once I was somebody
there was gravity, I had weight
there was an inside and an outside
now I'm nobody
gravity has gone, I seem weightless
no borders, formless
where is the past or future
there are not even objects left
where has time and space gone
there is only suchness
beyond all words
flying like a bird

look after your body

it's the temple of the spirit

but be clear, it's only the temple

when you become identified with the temple

you've forgotten the heart

when the spirit no longer shines

the structure is but an empty shell

give the body its place

an expression of the ultimate

and let it express the ultimate

let there be space
space in your life
in your mind
space to be quiet
discover space in your eyes, in your brain
open yourself to space
in spaciousness you're open to the unknown
spaciousness is welcoming you
your home without borders

the I you talk about is an imposter
who has taken up residence in the palace
he may act the part
looking like a prince
see through the illusion
vanquish the ghost
see who is really there

being nobody

it may not sound very enticing

but hey, without all that me stuff

you can fly

there's spontaneity

there's action free of all encumbrances

no more actor, no more sufferer

no more mr or mrs somebody

just the dance of life

the tide ebbs and flows
the seasons follow one on another
people fall in and out of love
it's a magical world
yes do explore it
but until you explore the explorer
you will go round in circles
never discovering your home
lost in a transitory show
never knowing the ultimate perceiver
of this ever-changing landscape

you don't have to be a victim of all the mind unleashes
fears and fantasies
all that erupts in the mind
that takes you down endless byways
take your stand in the I am
observe the scenery from here
the comedies and tragedies
you don't have to let it engulf you
you're just an observer of the film
until there is no film
not even an observer
only peace itself

through effort you can climb the mountain
or obtain a master's degree
you may need effort to know what you're not
but to know who you are needs no effort
it's beyond the realms of body and mind
only live in openness

the train can make progress along the railway track
the butterfly can migrate to Africa
but for the Self there is no progress
how can the permanent
outside time and space progress
it ever is
seeing the illusion
leave aside your progress
freedom is here and now

come in the door without an agenda

with no intention or purpose

come in your nakedness

you may be surprised what you find in yourself

and in the other

free of yourself

you will also free the other

let die all that's personal
let die your past
the male, the female
let die all purpose
all effort
let die silence into Silence
let die meditation into Meditation
let die yourself into the Self

every perception, thought or object
has its reality in consciousness
bring back every perception
and let it die back from whence it arose
but how do I do that
you don't need to
just see that every perception is time bound
and dissolves in presence, which is beyond time
you only need to allow it
and recognise that objectless moment

that which has no name or form
and cannot be perceived
expresses itself in every name and form
in every perception
it takes nothing to itself
but bestows reality on all

I am pure consciousness
stay with this thought
absorb it deeply
let it pervade your being
don't embroider it with association
stay with it untouched by any other thought
until even this thought dies
leaving only This

the words of truth have been heard
and recognised in yourself
now let every experience, every thought
be seen in this light
a reminder to confirm the reality
until it shines of itself

don't sacrifice this moment
for another moment
don't rush the washing up
to go to meditation
let the washing up be your meditation
the beauty is to be found here and now
and not in some imagined dream

renounce the world
go and live in the Himalayas
find a monastery away from it all
shield yourself from those enticing eyes
and search for peace
the only problem is there is still a you
and in any case what you call the world
is not other than the Self

consciousness likes to play its games

acting like a schoolboy

like a squirrel scampering around a tree trunk

like the blue sky in summer

and even taking your own name

and acting out your drama

but have you not seen beyond the mirage

and seen who is the real actor here

enticed by all the objects of the world
the mind is never still, blown by every wave
but when orientated towards truth
there's nothing for the mind to hold
it knows reality is beyond it
when the mind comes to clarity
you live in stillness
the world has dissolved

what joy it is to know

that there is nothing but consciousness

that all that is seen and heard

is within consciousness

there is no outside or inside

there is no division

no you or I

that all has its essence in consciousness

that all you ever experience is consciousness

66

now you've come to know the Self
don't try to be the saint
ripples from the old me
may spring forth
embrace them
give them their own space
so they can dissolve in the ocean

leave aside all, relax
float on the surface
sink deeper and deeper into the ocean
down to the bottom of the sea
relax, leave aside all
sink deeper and deeper through the seabed
until you reach the utter depths
the ground of being

feel your verticality
from earth to the heavens
piercing through time and space
in the nowness of eternity
ending fragmentation
the walls have crumbled
I once lived in my head
now my head is in me
I once lived in a body
now the body lives in me
I used to live in the world
now the world lives in me
the walls have crumbled
I'm nowhere to be found
I'm everywhere to be found

you may get a glimpse of the sacred
when you visit the temple
but you don't need to look outside
when the sacred is within
and within all

you may arrive at the stillness of the mind
to the absence of thought
but this absence is still a perception
Silence is other than the absence
or presence of thought
it ever is
and nothing can disturb it

fear of silence
having to face myself
my agitated mind and erratic breathing
it's all too much
let me escape back to my ceaseless activities
and hide from myself

deeply relax your eyes, brain and whole body
here you're free of all agitation
of volition and direction
of all desire and wanting
free of yesterday and tomorrow
you come to the timeless
the Now

let the silence absorb you
let the stillness dissolve you
no, this is not oblivion
here lies your real birth
beyond all form

it may appear mundane
but it depends who's looking
love only sees love
the sacred only sees the sacred
consciousness only sees consciousness
discover the real looker
and all is revealed

there is just functioning
why invent a functioner
ultimate reality is functioning
why interfere
when we don't, the ultimate functions
otherwise we are distorting life
breaking the flow of the river
clouding the clear sky
stand aside
and let life function

the words of the wise one
are not the reality
but if you let them pervade
every cell of your being
their perfume resonate through your life
the old me will dissolve
and reality beckon

walking through the old English garden
alighting on the peony
its beauty shared without reserve
to all that pass its way
asking nothing in return
the joy is here for all
that would but see

you've walked through the Garden of Eden
but did you stop five minutes to look
the cello was playing the adagio
but where were you
you've been given the gift of life
but have you opened it to look inside
when your time comes you may wonder
why was I always too busy
to listen

I've been knocking at your door
but no answer
I'm there in your deep sleep and in between thoughts
but you take me as nothing
I enter your dreams
but you soon forget me
I create road blocks in your life
but you barely turn your head
what more can I do
perhaps before your final departure
you will look my way
a pity to wait till then

let me introduce myself

at the moment I'm invisible to you

we can't shake hands

but persevere, and I will unveil who I am

you may get a glimpse of me between your thoughts

I will become more and more present to you

you may feel as if I'm behind you

welcoming all that is perceived

later you may see me in front of you

manifesting in all things

then you will come to know me as yourself

free yourself from the tyranny of time
fly free of its domain
it's no more than a thought
welcome eternity in the moment
consciousness does not belong to time
what you are is timeless
free of a past or a future
free of all that time presents
like the tern, fly free

the evening sunset
a Monet painting
the laughter of a child
beautiful moments
reminding us of our own beauty
but every moment is wet with its source
every moment Consciousness is
no need to search elsewhere

sitting by the waterfall with headphones on
walking through the forest lost in your gadget
ignoring the gift that would speak with you
living in a shell isolated from the whole
encased in a body-mind
unavailable to the song of the divine

84

when you walk in the woods
leave your mind at home
divest yourself of luggage
go naked
let the song of the birds
resonate in every cell of your being
touch life all around you
let it touch you
lose yourself in the greenery
no you, only life

searching for your real nature
cannot be a side show, a curiosity
not some part-time job
unless there is passion
it will be of no avail
you have to be on fire with your questions
unless the fire is burning bright
it will not destroy the illusion

the words of the teacher
where do you hear them
on the surface of your brain
or do they permeate
every atom of your being
do you hear them for a moment
or hear their echo pervading your whole life
no longer words
but the unspeakable reality

sitting by the pond on a cloudy evening
reading a book
suddenly a break in the clouds
the light dazzling
on the water, in my eyes
my book laid aside
in wonderment
filling my whole being

our smiles met
barely a second
two strangers
my heart danced its way home
no longer strangers
our beings one
wordless, timeless

I have now eliminated
all that you told me that I am not
body, senses and mind
the five sheaths
now nothing remains
I'm left with a blank
I still do not know the Self
only nothingness
but who is the seer of this nothingness

who am I
don't go to memory
it won't answer your question
it's just another thought
but if you allow the timeless
the answer will arise

the joy of hearing birdsong at dawn
the evening colours in the sky
but then it fades
what is this joy
is it from the child's laughter
or the harmony of the raga
no, it's always there, it's you
it's never gone away
the smile, the colours
are just reminding you what always is

sitting on a park bench
the sunlight through the branches
her head resting on his shoulder
her eyes closed
now in utter contentment
but without the park bench
the sunlight or a shoulder to lean on
there is also utter contentment now
if you are willing to discover it

a termite trying to control the Amazon in flood
a dolphin trying to divert the ocean current
you trying to manipulate the vastness of life
see the absurdity
why not just flow with the stream

94

do I not have free will to choose what I wish
but how can an imaginary I have any freedom at all
so if I have no freedom is my life already destined
but how can an illusion have a destiny
only free of your vivid imagination lies freedom

strip yourself of everything you know
your name, your form
your age, your gender
nationality
your personality
even your mind
come to nothing
and rest in the joy

when you see beauty
you, yourself are the beauty
when you feel love
you, yourself are the love
let it infuse your being
and let it radiate all that surrounds you

don't make an object of the moon
let it shine within you
don't make an object of the world
feel it as your manifestation
don't make an object of silence
be the Silence

imagine all you own disappears
imagine you have no past or future
imagine all your thoughts disappear
now imagine your body has disappeared
now remain as you are
fully present

be aware of the flow of your breath
let it come to you
let it go
free of volition
let the breath breathe you
now feel the space after the exhale
wait here for the gift of the inhale
abide here in this empty moment
not a moment, but timeless
not empty, but fullness

100

you may listen to all the teachers
read a hundred books
searching for what is missing
but if you only allowed the stillness
to give the answer

let the feeling of your body awaken
without thought or memory
let the warmth melt the solidity
feel it as vibration
feel it pervading the space all around you
feel yourself global
no border
one with space
living in openness

coming to tranquillity, equipoise, peace, silence
don't stop here
go deeper
where no words can go
to the inexpressible

when the desire arises
can you just observe it
as if from afar
doing nothing about it
giving it no hold
and let it fade away

look without a looker
see everything as for the first time
fresh, new
you may be astonished

I'm searching for a guru to teach me
can you help me
but if you're so busy searching
how will the guru find you
but how will she find me
only after deep inner reflection
only in the intimacy of your silence

give yourself to the night
take nothing with you
your eyes sinking back
let fall away all the dust of the day
abandon all you hold
body and mind
enter the darkness
where only peace sings

take your stand on the mountain top
view the world from here
see your fears and anxieties
welcome them
here you remain untouched by all that arises
let every perception die in the mist
leaving only presence

the autumn leaf falls at my feet
now nearing time to say goodbye
allowing the expression of a body-mind
to merge back with the earth
in thankfulness
to have walked in the forest and seen the moon
to have been able to breathe and see the light
yet knowing nobody was ever born
or will ever die

let this ocean of silence bathe your body and mind
let it bathe all you hear and see
let every word you use come from this ocean
live and be this ocean of silence
hear and breathe it every moment

About the Author

Billy is a qualified yoga teacher. He studied with many teachers in a wide variety of approaches. In 1982 he met Jean Klein who introduced him to Yoga in the Kashmir Tradition. He worked closely with him for many years attending his seminars in England, Holland, France and the United States.

Billy has published a book which presents these teachings: *Yoga in the Kashmir Tradition: the art of listening* (New Sarum Press).

He's also the author of *The Mirage of Separation* (New Sarum Press) a collection of poems and prose written from a non-dualistic perspective, covering subjects that include identification, desire, time, the spiritual path and silence.

CONVERSATIONS ON AWAKENING

Interviews by Iain and Renate McNay

Conversations on Awakening features 24 unique accounts of Awakening all taken from transcripts of interviews made for conscious.tv.

Some of the interviewees are renowned spiritual teachers while others are completely unknown having never spoken in public or written a book.

These conversations will hopefully encourage you, inspire you, and maybe even guide you to find out who you really are.

Conversations on Awakening: Part One features interviews with A.H Almaas, Jessica Britt, Sheikh Burhanuddin, Linda Clair, John Butler, Billy Doyle, Georgi Y. Johnson, Cynthia Bourgeault, Gabor Harsanyi, Tess Hughes, Philip Jacobs and Igor Kufayev.

Conversations on Awakening: Part Two features interviews with Susanne Marie, Debra Wilkinson, Richard Moss, Mukti, Miek Pot, Reggie Ray, Aloka (David Smith), Deborah Westmorland, Russel Williams, Jurgen Ziewe, Martyn Wilson and Jah Wobble.

Published by White Crow Books.
Available from Amazon in ebook and paperback format and to order from all good bookstores.
Part one: p.282, ISBN: 978-1786770936
Part two: p.286, ISBN: 978-1786770950

www.conscious.tv

A Selection of Books in Print from New Sarum Press

By Billy Doyle—*Yoga in The Kashmir Tradition* (2nd Edition), *The Mirage of Separation*

By Jean Klein—*Transmission of the Flame, The Ease of Being, Open to the Unknown, Beyond Knowledge, The Book of Listening, I Am, Who Am I?, Be Who You Are, Living Truth*

Real World Nonduality—Reports From The Field; Various authors

The Ten Thousand Things by Robert Saltzman

Depending on No-Thing by Robert Saltzman

The Joy of True Meditation by Jeff Foster

'What the...' A Conversation About Living by Darryl Bailey

The Freedom to Love—The Life and Vision of Catherine Harding by Karin Visser

Death: The End of Self-Improvement by Joan Tollifson

Awake in the Heartland by Joan Tollifson

Glorious Alchemy—Living the Lalita Sahasranama by Kavitha Chinnaiyan

Collision with the Infinite by Suzanne Segal

Looking Through God's Eyes by Han van den Boogaard

The Genesis of Now by Rich Doyle

Fly Free by Dami Roelse

Here, Now, One by Terry Moore

www.newsarumpress.com

Printed in Great Britain
by Amazon